Also by Steven Luria Ablon

Poetry

Tornado Weather
Flying Over Tasmania
Blue Damsels
Night Call

Non-Fiction

The Development and Sustenance of Self-Esteem in Childhood

Feelings: Explorations in Affect Development and Meaning

Dinner in the Garden

poems by
Steven Luria Ablon, MD

To Gridth

One

Two

Three

"It is out of the dailiness of life that one is driven into the deepest recesses of the self."

Stanley Kunitz

One

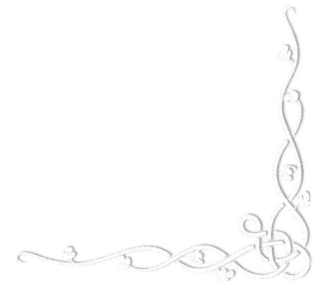

Mother Tongue

Before sleep my mother read me
Babar stories, one book each night,
the pictures bright as pastries.

*"In the great forest a little
elephant is born. His name is Babar."*
Sitting beside me in my bed,

my mother sang Sur le Pont d'Avignon,
l'on y danse, l'on y danse smelling
of exotic intimacy, *Chanel Cinq*, she said.

When Babar's mother was shot,
I cried on my pillow, and she stroked my hair.
Babar found a new mother who

bought him clothes, showed him
the elephant he was in the sun
marbled mirror. When there were

no more books, she read *Babar* to me
in French, that soft sibilance and so
I could begin to learn my mother tongue.

Years later just home from college
riding in her red Mercury
on the Henry Hudson Parkway

her hair tied up in an Hermes scarf.
I was Babar beside her again
in our happy France.

Lunch at the Knife and Fork Inn

My grandmother selects from the menu
two-pound lobsters, one for each of us.
Even before they come she ties too tight
the plastic bib around my neck,

smooths my collar, pats my cowlick down.
While we wait, I study her thin white hair,
the tiny shafts to her scalp, her skin
so wrinkled on her fragile wrists.

On large oval plates waiters bring them,
blushing red, black spots, dead. Ferociously
she works her cracker and her seafood fork,
finding the route to the delicate caves

until just bare shell and cartilage remain.
I crack the back, rip the meat from tail,
suck each cutter claw, and scrape the sacs
eating all the roe. She says, *a cruel fact,*

you are eating unborn lobsters. I look down
at my plate, think dying baby lobsters,
my grandmother's body torn by time. We sit
in silence, the ocean weeping on endless sand.

Appendectomy

Nurse Yamaguchi gathers up
her bag, winks at me. She thinks
we're friends but we are not.

Will she return in the morning,
wash me, turn my shoulders,
peppermint soap stinging?

Would she take me home,
read me *The Wizard of Oz*,
how Dorothy found her way
home at last? She pulls

my sheets too tight, restrains
me from following her home,
walks the hall like a tugboat.

I'm the barge heaped with coal and fish,
steely, calm on the end of a great rope.
Was I hungry? Didn't I want some soup?

Barbershop

I climb up into the leather swivel chair.
Vito says, Hello young man, the sheet
all whiteness hovering, breathless, settles
on my shoulders like a great white swan.
He combs my hair flat, both of us looking
at me in the mirror. He measures me up.

Now the clippers hum, mow my scalp
to half an inch of bristle, like a Sunday lawn.
Hair tumbles around me like a waterfall
onto the floor. A dab of Brylcream,
a dusting of talc on my neck. He cuffs me
on my back. *Good work,* he says, my smock

flourished off with his hand. I jump down
say, *thank you,* reach deep into my left pocket
for the five-dollar bill, into the other for
the crumpled dollar tip. The reward toys
are piled in the window. I take for my own
a black Oldsmobile. I know my cars.

Patty's Doll

First remove the doll's swivel arms,
like wishbones hard to break. Legs are easier
snapped from their ball joints, then pause
to admire the dismemberment, my medieval

transgression, each limb attached by rope
to a horse. What will my sister say when
she finds Eloise? Will she now never walk
into my room, never take my toys, never

sit so beautiful while I pick my nose?
Will there be jail for me? I buy a new doll
with an ermine coat, tell my sister Eloise
is studying abroad. Jasmine has taken her place.

When Class Ends

In grade school the bell, an alarm forgotten,
kids pour down the steps spreading

like dust motes into the city, for me
a crosstown bus and up Madison.

In high school the round wall clock,
clicks ten of four, hours playing baseball

and the walk down the hill in the Bronx
to Al's Variety. Sitting at the counter,

5 cents an egg cream, each thick glass
washed in a communal sink of suds,

all of us drinking from one well,
and college, graduate school, hoping

if I keep going to class will there be no end,
no dismissal, never to return, no walk home?

Piano Lesson

Shy eyed woodcock brooding over Wheaties
Miss Saperstein ringing the doorbell,

composing herself on the bench, her tight
red skirt stretching above her thin

metronomic knees. Positioning the music
on the stand like a dozen red roses,

flexing her shoulders so her sweater pulled
against her breasts. I was her disappointment.

Practice might have helped but one note sounded
like every other. I was a dreamer,

no attention to the lesson, no talent.
While she talked Mozart's Piano Sonata

I was thinking about Henry Miller,
The Tropic of Capricorn, how he seduced

his teacher. That night I was Reinhold,
captain of the steamer Pago Pago,

carrying bananas, rum and fugitives
from jungle ports, my straw hat, white linen

jacket, red suspenders. I am the owner
of the largest banana plantation

in the hemisphere. I buy drinks
for everyone, paying for the band.

Farm House Pond

I found a beaver wet with the slick
of its oil, pug nose pointing to fleeing
clouds. I found an otter making
scattered patterns in its wake,
a muskrat crunching submerged roots,

two red winged blackbirds lifting
their feet in a strange symphony.
I found a blue heron whose tiny eyes
stared unblinking, bound to me,
and four green willows beside

a wooden bridge across the water's
girth where I'd come for fat catfish
that cruise the muddy bottom but
found the trout my father stocked
ten barrels full, leaping loops in air,

the Titicus River running off with them.
In August, my cousins come for me
to show them how to wade the banks
which were thick with cat o' nine tails,
green helmeted pantomime pods.

My hunting knife in hand I taught them
how to make their torches, to slash stems
diagonally, to stir my can of kerosene,
ignite them with my Zippo. I marched
our little band, torches hissing, raising steam.

The Lessons of Ice Cream

I was too reticent, unflavored,
shy with girls to ask them to go out
for ice cream, plain vanilla in simple

grade school life. Little did I know
of the vanilla orchid, or its pollinator,
the Melipona bee. I believed in

chocolate with sprinkles, a banana
split with a cherry, whipped cream.
By senior year it was sherbert,

all sophistry, and maybe I would
date only girls who liked mango, or
a scoop of strawberry in a metal dish.

Summer

That summer I wanted to be a poet
lying on the couch, writing three lines,
crossing one out, clipping it in the yellow
notebook, weeding the flower bed,

a pencil behind my ear to write about
worms, their endless beginnings and
endings, at the beach, a conch and
a dozen pearl pink lines. This happy life,

no hurry, no product, nothing beyond
revision, a new idea in every moment,
knowing nothing until it is written and again
no beginning, no ending, knowing nothing.

The Pine Barrens

Transfixed in soundless
space, alert for the first
gust of morning, a fawn

passed shadows in uncut
grass. *Too dangerous*
my grandmother said,

so none of us ever went,
all those summers with
my cousins, girls who

only wanted to play hopscotch.
I had to walk the boardwalk
alone, Taylor Pork Rolls all

salt and smoke, played mini golf,
and beat the course, collected
tickets at Skee Ball, rolled

each ball into that center circle,
saved them for my future.
I could catch crabs. I could dive

under the highest waves at the
impervious edge of the surf.
I would never see that fawn.

After the Storm

Foliage dropping with each gust, each rain
and at the reservoir I run by a man

who in his blindness windmills his hands,
asks me could I find his glove. I see

it raveled, black next to the dog
that worried me at first sight across

the dimpled water. Was it the tense
back haunches, one ear laid back,

trembling? I ask him to move the dog.
He says it is a guide dog. I pick

the glove up, hand it to him,
afraid of his blindness. I run on,

asking myself why so fearful, full of
mistrust or did I see animal to animal,

bedlam in the dog's black eyes?
I think of the fox coat trembling

when my Aunt walked, the head,
the claws frozen, a look of agony,

the iron trap fixed to the tiny
bed of leaves, the no escape.

Student Exchange

For me it was a tent in Corsica,
savage sand turning to wood

shavings, flies mating with flies,
the mandolin moon iridescent,

boys digging for lost jewelry, and I
so tired only the burning sun

woke me, the end of my voyage,
everything spent, all you needed

was bus fare to the airport, sweat stained
survival, a cup of luck, trust in others.

Staten Island Ferry

A full moon ladders the bay.
I am on a date, my back
against the railing, she leans

into me, watching the lights
of Wall Street roll in the sky.
And I think I see Miss Wing,

my fourth-grade teacher.
I loved her ankles as thin
as a fife. She told me

I would lead a scholar's
life, exotic and remote
like the Shalimar perfume

she bathed our class
in every day. But I was
busy becoming the center

fielder for the Yankees, loping
under a parabolic fly ball,
knowing I would arrive at

the place of perfect intersection.
Oh fate, let Miss Wing look up,
let her smile on me again.

The Trout

All of his life of hiding, riding,
embraced by waters' fast flow,
red rainbows enamel his scales.

I watch him swim, then tug,
then reel, exhaust him in,
wrenched into air, his eyes

wide open, his tail drumming
the sky. And didn't I catch
the four grasshoppers

in my bare hand, and force
my barbed steel
hook through the belly?

I cast the long loop of line
into the drift that
froths and swirls.

I now stand uneasy
on that shaded bank
where my catch struck hard.

Horse at Salem Farms

Uncombed, dirt living on his ears,
a chestnut horse walks across
the field to me. Eye to eye,
he nuzzles my heart with his nose.
I scratch his neck, separate

congealed clumps of mane. We've met
before, in a dream, some knowledge
known but not. He watches as I climb
under the barbed wire behind the path.
Did a boy lonely under the boughs

of apple trees curry and brush
this horse every day, polish the white
flash on his forehead and with just a rope
halter ride him bareback across pastures
into the pond, lonely horse, lonely boy?

Because My Last Name Begins With A

A is always first, always anxious,
always armed. So I never learn

to improvise, always on the line.
When we went to the park each day

in kindergarten the teacher called on me
to cross Eighth Avenue, cars not even

slowing yet. In second grade I had to sit
in the front row under Miss Munson's

blue hawk eyes, first to touch the turtle
in its bowl. Every sixth-grade boy tried

to beat my hundred-yard dash.
By high school time never ran out

before I was called to translate
a passage from Balzac, "*There is*

no such thing as a great talent
without great will power." It wasn't

until sophomore year Tom Aaron
moved to New York from Guam.

By then I wanted to be first, to get it
done, to take the risk, set the standard.

Dressing Up

I wear the watch, gold work thin as leaf veins
my father bought in Hungary after the war
in which he was stationed at a desk in Philadelphia.

I wear my uncle's cuff links, solid gold dice,
a six on every side from his tough guy life,
the Jew boxer sent to an air force base in Kerala.

I bought a t-shirt like Maggio in "*From Here
To Eternity*," wore it to the movies, leaned over,
whispered over the credits to my wife,

"*Only my friends can call me a little wop!*"
I bought a Yankee hat to shade my eyes
as I lope deep into centerfield among

the monuments tracking that baseball
until it crashes a perfect fit in my glove.
I smoke a Meerschaum pipe my professor

in college smoked when I came to him
for extra help. When I finish school, I will
dress in a doctor's coat, unblemished white.

Slack Tide

Spartina, mud,
hermit crabs
hunting
camouflage,
rock red
stirring
the surface.
Uncertainty
rising.
In that
uncovering,
all will be
changed.

Pitch-Backs

They come back
to me with a twist,

like bad dreams.
Bad throws dribble off,

no warning.
Black strings ratcheted

to the frame
and there is always

a response,
tireless, willing

until dusk,
without reprimand

without love,
endurance.

Cleveland Ohio, Medical School

Suddenly a trumpet skulks incendiary
on my downstairs neighbor's vine.
I am thief of moonlight among
the boisterous bloom. With

the penknife I always wanted
and my father gave me when
I was 12, I cut a sliver of the stem,
with a spoon, turn the earth,

and between two fingers press
that stem deep in the dark earth,
a lip hanging in the air. With fishing line
I tie it gently to my fence on the far side

of our 3-decker where my neighbor
cannot see. My pace is slow, my crime
an avalanche. I water my vine
twice a week, search for root hairs

of my nurturance. My vine widens,
winds around the stave. By June I see
three orange flowers unscroll.
I am the thief of beauty.

Elective in China: The Temple of Heaven, Beijing

Everything moves honey-slow here,
the peach trees, the rhododendrons,
the people on all the benches,
and on all the chairs. At a wooden table
near the entrance, a Chinese girl with short
red hair slams down four cards, takes crumbled
money from the hands of a sanguine man.
They play on. By the red stairway bridge
in a wheelchair a man plays a two-string fiddle.
Beside him a woman cradles a full moon
banjo. On the makeshift stage two men sing
and respond, their voices great claps
of thunder, dynasties resounding.

I stand by the west celestial gate
watching couples dancing on the grass.
A woman leaves the shadow of solemn
cypress, puts both hands out for me to dance.
She wears orange cotton gloves, a blue dust mask.
I like the scent of her, the radishes
and eggplant on her breath, and there is a coarse
blue vein stumbling down the middle of her
forehead.
We turn and turn. Sixty years ago, my mother
taught me to foxtrot, lifted my arm like
a drawbridge under which she'd twirl. I am
that drawbridge, the calm that darkens
among the light. We dance.

Sunday Morning

I am slowing down in the lane
beside the parked cars

watching for a brake light,
watching for someone reaching

for keys. I am surveying
the other side of the street,

a motion that demands a U-turn,
a motion that demands backing down.

The spot too small, the spot not
small at all. I am all back and forth.

I hook slide into home, safe,
my radio murmuring Beethoven.

I blow my horn and I am
complacent in the driver's seat.

Newbury Street

Crickets are calling the end of summer
when a woman in a starched white shirt,
black skirt that clings, hurries toward me.
She lost her purse, lives on the Cape
and needs money for the bus. She tells me
this is so awkward but it's late, her family
is visiting in Canada. Could I lend her some
money?

Such a nice woman, forty dollars should do it.
She walks toward the bus station and my sons
say to me, *"Dad, don't you live in the world?*
She's a con artist." I liked her black sandals,
her perfect pink nail polish. I'd give her
the money again. Won't the Messiah
come as a beggar to save us?

Playing Texas Hold 'em With You

Bluffing is a way of life as
easy as jumping the breakers.

I play for dollars on the table.
The hole, two down: king, king,

don't show my cards, press them
flat face down. Flop three cards

ten, five, jack. A single card,
the turn, a ten. Now stand guard,

don't give luck away. Calculate
what's certain, what's possible,

pretending what you have is
better than it is. The last card

on the table, ten, is the river
you cross only once. No return.

Jimmy Fund Benefit Auction

I used to bring you sun brewed tea from the farm
and both of us lobsters from the stand you love.
I've loved you since the summer I was a medical
student and you took tickets at the loop de loop.
That summer you asked me what I love about you,
wanting me to say your mind, your soul.

But it was your body I wanted, to ride the Ferris
wheel again, to suspend us at the top.
Now we've eaten our shrimp and razor clams
and you raise your hand, call out the top bid,
lean one hip into mine, sway, say, *I feel so good
I could break someone's heart. Going once.*

You are bidding on a day for me in the dugout
at Fenway Park. I hold your arm back. The auctioneer
stares me down. *Leave her alone, let her make
her own decision!* It's guilt I guess that makes me
hold your arm down for the last bid. The second we lost
I knew I would regret this forever, you who hold nothing back.

Just Married

I don't have to call you two weeks
ahead anymore to ask if you are free
Saturday night. Would you like to go
to the movies? We hold hands

until your arm falls asleep and you place
your hand on my thigh and we split
a box of Goobers, tear off the top, pour
the brown kernels in our palms

and you leave the last kernels for me,
my two fingers digging them from the bottom.
At home it is early, time to make love,
time for the long sleep after.

Two

Life with My Father

Every moment crisis
or crisis withheld -
out of bed to pee,
tempting a stroke,

to hang pajamas
on the hook, a fall,
a broken hip, step
over the lintel into

the shower, slipping
on ceramic tile,
spread toothpaste
on brush, polishing,

polishing. Each ordinary
act a miracle, each
wave on the beach
and everywhere, sharks.

The Murdered Moles

How many nights has he
put on his boots to walk
the lawn by lantern light,
stamped down bulging burrows,
forcing flat the pressure plate,
pulling compact coiled springs
to load the blades?

When moles return, they tunnel,
raise the ground, release
those spears.
Mornings he checks which ones
untouched, which ones are sprung,
moles crimsoning the grass
dying deep underground.

Let There be a Barbecue When I Die

Throw a party for the friends who sat
for hours in the kitchen eating bagels
and lox and all the pretenders who call
each time to say they missed me, come
now for my death as much as for their survival.

Let it be a barbecue at the beach, play
Jimmy Buffet's "Cheeseburger in Paradise."
Heaven on earth with an onion slice.
Not too particular, not too precise.
I'm just a cheeseburger in paradise.

Let my grandchildren read, one by one,
their favorite poem of mine. Let Luke read
the one I wrote about his hamster dying
on Christmas, let Cam read *My Heart*
and my wife, *Just Married*. In the living room

show the Red Sox World series victories,
the last out settling in the pitcher's glove
every player hugging, crying. Let it be
pulled pork and ribs, Malpeque oysters,
steamed clams, everything I love.

Said and Unsaid

"That distant afternoon when his father took him to discover ice."
Gabriel Garcia Marquez

Most things I leave unsaid
but my son leaned over

the arm rest, he and I,
on the way to Venezuela

to catch bone fish and tarpon.
Oh, Dad, I love you. I sat

stunned, grateful. *I love you.*
You're a wonderful son

I say and think of my father
who used to say; *You are such*

a smart aleck, Steve,
what's wrong with you?

The Times

My father hunts the obituaries
for friends. Every time I visit
he wakes me to go to the end
of the farm's gravel drive.
He stands at my door knocking,

knocking. In a second I am
awake, throw on my clothes,
help him feel his way down
his front steps, open the door
to see if we need coats.

He is quick limping to the car.
I pilot him the one hundred yards
for the paper. We are too early
to discover the name, someone
he'll know he has outlived.

All My Uncles, All My Aunts

Everyone drinking gin and tonic,
everyone smoking Camels,
Canasta on my parents' porch,
the sound of Chinese dancers
snapping fans. I was 10, crawling
in the thick of grass of Connecticut
chasing the fireflies that climb
the fallen split crab apples.
A black bird waits to decide.
The magnolia blooms late
in August wanting to be white

when everything else is gone.
My father wanted fast cars,
hugged his Lamborghini close
on country roads. Power, more
than he could use. My father
always parked on Main Street
at the hardware store, at the
green grocers wanting people
to envy his rich man's car.
He had bested his father, still
working his used car lot in Ohio.

At the Pool

He wears wool trousers to the pool,
a dress shirt, a tweed jacket
to the gym where he swims
three times a week, undresses,
one hand on the metal locker

for balance, finds his swim suit
and goggles, faces the ladder,
lowers himself slowly,
his arms, his calf muscles taut until
he lets loose and drops

into the pool, pushes off,
falls forward eyes blinking water.
Every muscle tense I wait for him
to emerge slow as a manatee. He swims
two laps hands falling heavily in water,

each stroke submerged too long.
The lap swimmers get out of his way,
leave the lane for him. I walk along
out of his sight, toes gripping the grout
between tiles. An attendant prepares

a lounge chair, spreads a sheet,
folds a towel for his feet. A man,
white curly hair on his head, on his chest
comes to sit on the end of his chair,
asks what to do about a child he never

knew he had. My father shakes his hand,
says, *it could be a blessing, a grandchild?*
Swimmers walk by, a man with a cane
sits down, asks about a bad loan.
My father says, *I will quote Polonius*

*even though he is a fool: "Neither a borrower
nor a lender be, For loan oft loses both itself
and friend."* These are my father's office hours,
his exercise, his putting on of socks,
one trembling leg at time. See you later boys.

At Le Perigord, on His 95th Birthday

The same old waiters tremble as they plate
Escargot and Osso Bucco steaming.
He tells the Maître d' to leave chairs
for old friends who died slowly the way
his garden moss crept to shale. My father

drools as white as a flock of buntings
on his black turtleneck, all spice and scent.
Next, he orders Napoleons for all,
struggles with his fork to conquer Mille-Feuille,
and ruin the marbled fondant.

He knows the father of the Maître d',
how he came here from Algeria
hidden in a bale of hay, studied viola
at Juilliard. We talk among ourselves.
Though I keep an eye on him, my lodestar,

the tweed suit from my wedding hanging
loosely on his frame, the old blue tie
with nimbus moons, though I have bought him
a new one each year to match the gold
cufflinks shine. The hand that signals

for the bill is bold. He has no trouble
with the numbers, tips handsomely, all
the wines and corks. Trembling he pushes
himself up. I walk by his side
to steady him but he won't consent.

I Offer to Pick His Tie

From the closet where ties hang
like so many trout caught on the line,

I choose the purple with yellow
polka dots I bought on Third Avenue

for his birthday when I was ten.
It was made in Italy.

It cost me eight weeks' allowance.
The most garish tie of all, frayed

narrow between my fingers
from where he pulled it under

his collar to make a muscled
Windsor knot, the lining so loose

it drips like saliva. Yes, he's kept it.
I decide to put it back, choose red instead.

He Wants us to Watch the Yankees on TV

Once I wanted to be the amazement,
like Mickey Mantle, a grand slam
homerun! I stand, my father stands
slow as the moon lifts itself in the sky.

Unstable as he is he pokes the carpet
three times with his cane. Oh, to be winged
like a cockroach resistant to the end,
taking refuge in every shadow.

My father bends his face
to my ear, *I have no*
complaints. I don't want to do
what I can't do anymore.

Asleep in His Recliner

Like an un-watered flower his head
hangs down, his breathing stentorian.
It is nine in the morning, sun
blasts through the wide living room

where he will sleep for three more hours.
Before sunrise he woke and made his bed,
hospital corners like he taught me,
by dropping a penny, watching it bounce

on his blanket. It takes two hours
for him to dress, the wheels of his muscles
slow to turn, fifteen minutes to button

each cuff starched tight. Today in the den
he asks my wife to help. Pushed away from
any attention by sisters, independent as he
always was and I his proud, humiliated child.

Kipling

One eye dark with hemorrhaged blood,
my father watches sports all day,
wakes and watches more. He asks me
the score, who is at bat, how much

time is left. I beg him to let me buy
a new TV. Defiantly he says this one is fine.
After lunch my sister, Jen, and I drive to Best Buy,
choose the newest, brightest big screen TV,

lug it back. He is in the kitchen talking to Anna,
the housekeeper who straightens up his life
each day. She is telling him that her boyfriend
wants to marry her, a poor girl from Poland.

What can she offer him? And he begins to recite
the poem he read us when we were kids.
For the Colonel's Lady an' Judy O'Grady
Are sisters under their skins.

Family Holiday

In New Zealand on a vast sheep farm,
my brother, Rich, and I listen
to all that wool rustling at night.
In the hall to the bathroom

I meet my father. We laugh,
soldiers of the battle of the
prostates, the sweet bond
of paternity.

Later I hear him in the hall fumbling
for the door. The night-light
in his room, not enough. From bed
I listen for progress. The toilet lid

thrown up, the seat dropped like
thunder. Another sleepless night
and in the morning, I'll see how
he has wet the front of his pajamas.

Studying Old

At 98 my father observes his spine is condensed,
he has lost two inches. His appetite fails,
food has no taste. We go to the fridge,
he finds the bottle of infant supplement,
sits with me at the dinner table,

grips as hard as he can, unscrews the top,
drinks it down at once. For the first time
he does what he has been told,
eats like the good boy he never was.
On our walk, he studies every trembling

step afraid of patchy ground. I reach for
his arm. He pushes my hand away,
tells me the young and the old don't
like to be helped. We watch his college team,
Ohio State, games from this week, games

from years ago. I know these games but still
want to see them, and I want every detail again.
I attach the plug from my computer
to his phone, update his software:
his cloudy eyes, his trembling hands.

He cannot seem to make his way.
Just when I think he can't see what
I am doing he calls out
Steven, what have you done.
The wires were too delicate to change.

My Father at 100

Six of us eating lunch at a round table at the hotel
down the street. It is four short blocks but we need a car
for my parents, each of them folded into the back seat.

My father holds my wrist for the long walk to the table.
We order. He can't taste his food, can't hear our
conversation.
It's cold in the restaurant. My mother's shawl has fallen
from her shoulders. He reaches out, a shaking hand lifts
it back over her.

Tonight, twelve blossoms will fall from the
Rose of Sharon, that small tree in the garden
of my childhood. I used to gather them,
at dawn. More bloom remained, full beyond counting.

At their apartment, my parents nap together motionless
on their couch. I kneel on their bathroom floor, scrub
feces from between their tiles, wash my father's
trousers caked with food and drool. I wash his shirt
in the sink, hang it up to dry. Soon enough
the Rose of Sharon will be bare,
that great bouquet passing like endless waves.

Three

The Next Generation

They want to ride with us in the car,
want to sleep over every weekend,
eat popcorn, watch TV; they wish

they could live with us. We take them
for ice cream, as many rainbow
sprinkles as they want.

They keep us young, make lively
our household, get it right this time.
Didn't we go to every soccer,

every baseball game, watch
ballet recitals wedged into auditoriums?
Didn't we study biology and Latin?

They left for college one by one and
each came back to visit at Thanksgiving,
let us grill them about courses, friends.

They hug us, say they will see us soon.
We are peripheral to the grandchildren,
a vein, a capillary far from the heart.

The Great Ape

My granddaughter wants to be as close
as skin on an apple. She spreads her arms,
presses herself against glass. She loves him,

clucks, taps the glass until the gorilla rises,
legs powerful, effortless, swaggers to the glass,
opens his cavernous all pink mouth and with

a paw as big as a catcher's mitt whacks that glass.
Kate doesn't blink. Is she trusting, reckless, thrilled?
She feels safe behind glass. I am with her for now.

Central Park

A man kicks the Frisbee into air,
catches it on his elbow, spins it
on his finger like it was a ring

of Saturn. A shirtless gymnast
somersaults three benches
to where we sit. I float a dollar

into his hat. Kate in her stroller
laughs. We follow the sound
of a clarinet, find a black beret

playing, *When the Saints.*
Kate nods with the music.
I wheel her to the boat lake, lift her

out to the yellow forsythia,
the magnolia buds peaking white.
Both of us hungry for sensation.

May she always turn to see
the bright mechanics of the world,
the leaps of daring, the passion.

Teaching Luke to Swim

A puppy on my chest,
his breath soft as
this early summer night.
He will remember

this spindly fatigue
as stars swim beside him
this fragile night. He shivers.
I want him to float lighter

than an embryo.
With my cupped hand
I splash his back,
his shoulders of moon

blanched baby fat,
the cadence of water
enfolding his legs, his smile
glimmering like frost.

Hospital Bed

After the saline comes water
and five percent dextrose.
The intravenous has exhausted
his veins, all blood and bruises

between crying and sleeping.
The hell with waiting hours.
He's only two. Am I not a doctor?
I have stood by the bed of my wife

and all my grandchildren.
I know what space is best for growth.
When Luke wakes he'll say
he doesn't need to wash his face,

doesn't like the peppermint toothpaste.
By lunch I'll bring him a moon
shaped cookie, watch him soothe
the edge of his blanket between his lips.

Comfort

With saws, they've opened up my daughter's skull,
let out that whine that disputes stubborn bone
to find that minuscule aneurysm to annul.

I tell her children that we are on a scull
whose waters make our timbers groan
threaten pegs and glue of our very hull.

The youngest wakes too early as he mulls
snow that glides to earth in silent moan.
He shovels grief where there is no lull,

I want to comfort my grandchildren, to dull
my pain as fragile as ocean foam,
as wind buffets us like mocking gulls.

Bailey, the Dog

Hers is the dark black coat
abandoned on a street in
Nashville, who found a home

with us. She is a hound,
braying, leaping in air
when she sees the biscuit

I bring. She knows, too,
I am dog, a huskie in the snow,
a poodle studying medicine,

both of us sniffing the hundred
years of lilacs buried here.
When Maggie can't sleep,

she leaps in the bed,
rests her buttocks tight
against Maggie's flannel pajamas.

At Cold Springs Park

I push Paige highest in the swing.
At the top, she scissors her legs, leans
back, laughs, says higher. She is too small
to play soccer at her brothers' games.

I play with her on the sidelines
passing the ball between us like our secret.
When she grows up she will be a princess,
a mommy, lots of children and go.

I worry she will be a girlie girl
all reliant on others. No, it will
be she who'll run the fastest,
gather the ball, an arrow shot

from a bow ahead of the field,
all close and score, do a perfect flip,
two cartwheels, a shiny pink ribbon
dancing in her hair.

Watching Peter Pan on TV

As Wendy and the boys are leaving home
my spitfire wants to know if she can lose
her shadow. I think of my carbon atoms
scattering into space unknown. *No darling,*

I say, *you will never lose your shadow.*
She wants to fast forward past Captain Hook
even though he is my favorite as old as I am,
listening for the clock as I never did at her age.

Tinker Bell drinks poison to save Peter and grows
faint.
We begin to clap, to bring her back to life,
me turning away, wanting to cry, Maggie crying,
at the fall one so small, so loyal I know I can't save.

A Princess Birthday Party

Maggie is not going.
She doesn't want to dress up
like a princess. She wants

to be a Power Ranger. I ask her
what a princess does? She says,
I don't know but Power Rangers

save the world. My wife says
a princess is strong, noble and helps
govern and make laws. You can be a

princess and a Power Ranger
and save the world. My wife is helping
with homework, Egyptian history,

cooking dinner for the grandchildren,
driving car pool between seeing patients.
She is all princess, all Power Ranger.

Hawk Standing in the Road

Drinking from a rivulet
in asphalt, standing,
ten feet away from
Jack and me,

boldness beyond
reckoning. I ask,
Do you think
the claws could

carry us away?
No Pa, he says,
You'll die a long
time before me.

A Celtics Game

Jack has to go to the men's room.
We stand in line outside. A guy
behind us, draining a beer

from each hand, leans forward,
Kid how do you like the game?
I can barely hear him say, *good.*

Who is your favorite player?
Jack looks down at his shoes,
whispers, *Garnett.* The guy says,

Slap me five. Jack is at the urinal.
He unzips his fly, reaches in for
his penis. I keep watch. Others

come and go. Is he having a problem?
He hitches up his pants. I step forward,
tell him *wash your hands.* The man says,

See you Jack. He walks quickly
back to our seats. I am proud.
He survived being one of the guys.

Because

His life at home is black ice,
sudden bursts of anger,

unprovoked. I would do
anything for him, leave

my New York Times
on the couch, drink

the remains of my ice tea,
not lingering to watch mint

leaves from the garden
settle to the bottom like light

at end of day. I pick him up
waiting outside his house, drive

to Cleveland Circle Hardware
so I can ask the man at the counter,

one long gold earring cleaving
the air, and he disappears

in canyons of equipment
in search of Velcro. I buy four rolls,

enough for both of us, a mini flashlight,
and gummy bears. On the drive home

Cam asks if we can plan other trips.
We love how Velcro sticks things together.

Pacemaker

Cam stares at my hospital
bed, stares at the monitor.
He wants to learn what are
those blue lines that draw

hills and valleys, the voyage
of the blinking numbers
of my heart. He wants
to try the finger clip

that checks oxygen.
Next time I'll fix your heart,
bring my hammer
and saw. He hands me

his Blankie, a torn diaper
from when he was born.
Keep it, he says, puts it
in the middle of my chest

where he thinks my heart
is, peers deep into my eyes
the way he did at the Natural
History Museum when I

smoothed the tangled hair,
head to tail on the tarantula's
back, showed him how scary
could make him brave.

Early October

The pine planks at the beach house thirst from neglect
and there are cracks, chasms that glisten with algae,

splinters of wood protrude. This cool October day
and I am grinding back and forth with the coarsest

of sandpaper, whose sawdust streams toward heaven
in black gusts. There will be no splinters anymore.

No need for me to be the doctor here.

Pitching a Knuckle Ball

Life gripped too tight
or not tightly enough.
I never know what

the ball will do. I dig
my fingernails into
the leather seam,

rotate my shoulder
half way, pushing it
forward like closing

a door, cock my wrist,
release the ball just
when my arm turns down.

This pitching will take practice,
the ball so tough to hit,
maybe even impossible.

Buying a Mitt

Like tropical fruit the baseball mitts
hang the aisle of Modell's.
I pick one, push my hand into
leather, stiff, slow to yield.
Charlie reaches only half way
into the fingers. I show him

how to leave his middle finger
outside, to protect his palm.
I add to our basket a can
of Neatsfoot oil, tell him
how he'll have to massage
with a rag, circle upon circle

in the glove and he will
have to teach his sons,
and surely he will. I will
give him my complete 1984
set: Major League Baseball Cards,
all of these men also fathers in this world.

An Adventure With Charlie

Sitka, Alaska: his 13th Birthday

The glaciers are calving, flumes of ice,
mist lost in the berg strewn sea. I must
steady the kayak, secure a hand on each
gunnel, that synchrony of pull and push,
force the paddles deep enough to resist
the tide of the Inland Passage.

We net somnolent sea cucumbers from
the bottom, hold them limpid, liquefying
in our hands. At dusk we lower traps,
summon the crabs who migrate across
the ocean floor. The last day I lower line,
fifty feet for haddock, wait for that downward

draft, then reel them in, our hands cramped
gripping the handle. In the morning
Charlie tells me he dreams about
a gull cruising above seas learning
the inlets of survival in this world.
I kiss him and say, *Safe Passage.*

First Mate

As timorous as early summer corn
we are buying a boat.
Carter is aggressive questioning

the seller, making sure we have
an anchor that will hold no matter
how strong the current, and a paddle

if the motor fails, and, yes, two
gas tanks one in reserve prepared for emergency.
He asks me, *Do you think*

we need a depth finder so we won't
run aground? And I say, *yes,* even though
the salesman says he'd never heard

of this, such a small boat.
Can he be the first grandchild
to drive the boat? *Definitely*, I say.

Internecine

The waiter brings them cantaloupe-sized balls of
pizza dough as formless as Madagascar on the map.
The children throw it back and forth among themselves,
tear off pieces, steal from one another, offer the tiniest
pea to their father, my son-in-law, who tries to rope them in:

Put it down. Don't make such a mess. And so to distract them
I stick dough under my nose: *a big snot*, I say. I put a piece
in my ear. I fashion a grotesque beard until all of us are laughing.
But the kids only want to copy me in what I'm beginning to think
was my mistake. They make up a sudden vomit, a baseball cap.
The pizza finally comes. Have I ruined dinner? Or was it they?

Sleep-over

We sit at the table in our pajamas.
Because he misses his mom I'm warming
milk on the stove, then I walk him to bed,
rub his back, until he falls asleep.
It's two A.M. I stumble to my window
where a squad car radio is rumbling

in the driveway. Charlie has dialed 911.
I open the door, dissemble calm.
The officer with his grave face asks,
what is the trouble here?
We are his grandparents; he misses
his mother. I feel guilty as always.

My wife comes down in her robe stands
inside the door, Charlie bent against her
in tears, the baseball players on his pajamas
smiling in eternal sunshine. The officer
assesses us, nods at Charlie, leaves.
I am sorry grandparents are not safe enough.

By Daylight

My son-in-law returns everything;
blue Patagonia windbreaker, leather
knapsack for hiking mountain trails

but today I bought him a blazer
that comes with a free wrist watch,
numbers as big as a corner office with

a harbor view. And because
what is added matters most
he loves the jacket, slides it off

the hanger, one sleeve at a time,
studies himself in it before the full length
mirror, then carries it outside to try it on.

My Son's Old Room

Sun collects dust motes on his cedar desk.
I am as lonely as the curtains in his shuttered
windows. Everything seems gravitational:
the angst of the unplugged floor fan,
a basketball half inflated in a box,

a picture aslant of a quarterback long retired.
I feel like crying as I sit on his bed
but my phone rings and I take it from my pocket.
Carter is asking if I could be his caddy today.
I say, *Yes,* glad to be leaving his father's room.

I grab my blue Mink Meadows hat and meet him there.
I will heft his bag over my shoulders, pulling his clubs
like radishes from the earth. Now Carter swings.
The ball is a golden orb we follow into the green,
blank verse of an azure windless day.

Waking at 3 a.m.

I have to pee even though I don't.
I place my arms across my chest

like the Buddha, to hold myself here.
This is how Stinestsky will arrange

me in the coffin. I think I feel like dying,
scratch the sheet, digging, digging, helpless,

get up out of this bed, hear the rumble
of a landslide, stumble, run to high ground,

hold trees being uprooted, mud, dirt, roots,
boulders coming to submerge me,

pee and shake the earth off.
I don't see death, just white light,

colloidal granite grooves of sandstone,
outside consciousness, blood basted

in my hair. It will be one step too far
into the canyons kaleidoscopic.

Because the Menu has Changed

Press 1
to pay your bill.
Press 2
to enter the last four digits of your...
Press 3
To enter your married sister's maiden name
Press 4
for special offers.
Press 5
to hear the menu again.
Press 6
for possibilities.
Press 7
to start over.
Press 8
for the polar icecap
Press 9
for self-sufficiency.
Press 10
for Madagascar,
to talk to someone
with time on his hands.

My Mother

I choose three pair of socks from the bargain bin,
and a golf shirt to match the lilacs in her yard.
At the counter, she fumbles with the purse
I bought at the airport when I arrived.

The clerk looks hard at my mother's credit card,
studies the address, clears his throat, clears his
throat again. *When I was ten I played hockey
on your pond.* My mother nods politely.

I recognize that square chin, his blue eyes,
the boy who lived on North Street year-round.
I smile and shake his hand. *We used our hats
for hockey goals*, he tells my mother. He laughs.

I am embarrassed to feel the torque of social class.
My mother never watched us, never kept up
with local boys. She says, *Let's go*, tightens
her grasp on my elbow, smiles with self-control,

holds the edge of my car's green roof, turns
her back, falls into the blue well of the car seat,
an act of faith. I feel the planetary pull between us,
surprised she doesn't need me anymore.

Christmas

The hamster is dead!

I sprint to the boys' bedroom,
see him motionless in his cage,
his white coat ruffled like an ornament,
open the hinge, take him into my hand.

He is cold. I feel for a faded pulse in his neck,
listen at his mouth for shadow breath.
Dead. How many times have I pronounced
these words, in emergency rooms,

in ambulances, not knowing who had died
or who he was. All the children put on
their jackets and boots, come with me.
The ground annealed with a sheet of snow.

They stand around me as I put the hamster
in a dent in the earth, cover him
with desiccated leaves.
Merry Christmas, Hampie, Luke whispers.

Dinner in The Garden

In their hammocks my grown sons daydream
$\qquad\qquad\qquad$ their loves from when they were boys.

My daughter's in the swing among her ghosts. Each
$\qquad$ of us still
$\qquad\qquad\qquad$ fighting our own civil wars. The grandchildren
are barefoot, fragrant after
$\qquad\qquad\qquad$ baths, hiding and seeking

in the stone strewn
garden where ants $\qquad\qquad$ in three lines
navigate
the vagaries of foreground.

We will eat on the porch, $\qquad$ enough table for all,
$\qquad\qquad\qquad$ my wife bringing one plate after another
plied with every vitality.
$\qquad$ Last year I felled the oak.
$\qquad\qquad$ The first blow severed the bark,
$\qquad\qquad\qquad$ the second
spewed off fibrous filaments of youth.

Now we open the table umbrellas
$\qquad\qquad$ for us to be
in shadow,
$\qquad\qquad\qquad$ the leaves of the aspen trembling.
$\qquad$ I call my parents
$\qquad\qquad$ to see the fireflies,
$\qquad$ my mother in her carnelian robe,
$\qquad$ my father in his business suit,
$\qquad$ leaning on the Masai mahogany cane.

We watch the lights that blink
$\qquad\qquad\qquad$ like foreign cities across the wide

and pampered lawn— $\qquad$ mellifluous grid of
$\qquad\qquad\qquad$ a universe calling out

to protect us, the fireflies making
luminescence

within their bodies, $\qquad\qquad\qquad$ without heat.

Acknowledgements:

I am deeply grateful to my family and friends, whose love has sustained me during the writing of these poems. I am especially grateful to my wife, Gridth, my daughter, Kim, and son, Stuart, for their advice and guidance, to Shana Hill for her assistance with submissions and editing, and to Barbara Helfgott Hyett whose generosity as a poet and a person has helped me find my way to the heart of these poems, and to the community of the Monday Morning Poets, where some of these poems began.

Finally, my thanks to the editors of publications in which many of these poems originally appeared, some in earlier forms, some with different titles:

The Avalon Literary Review: "Life with My Father"

The Cafe Review: "Because My Last Name Begins with A," "Because Our Menu Has Changed," and "Waking at 3 A.M."

Crack the Spine: "Patty's Doll"

Encircle Publications: "Student Exchange"

Ginosko: "Mother Tongue," "Pacemaker," "Dinner in the Garden," "The Trout," and "Bailey, the Dog"

Happy Holidays Anthology: "Christmas"

The Invisible Bear: "Life with My Father"

The Main Street Rag: "The Hospital Bed"

Modern Poetry Quarterly Review: "Internecine"

The Piedmont Journal of Poetry & Fiction: "Appendectomy," "Never Found," "Jimmy Fund Benefit Auction," and "Playing Texas Hold 'em with You"

Riding Light: "All My Uncles, All My Aunts"

Third Wednesday: "Studying Old"

Silver Birch Press: "Lessons of Ice Cream"

Pear Drop: "Lunch at the Knife and Fork Inn"

West Trade Review: "Central Park"

Typehouse Literary Journal: "The Murdered Moles" and "Kipling"

You Are Here: "An Adventure with Charlie" and "Let There Be a Barbecue When I Die"

Steven L. Ablon has published four books of poems: **Tornado Weather**, (Mellen Press), 1993, **Flying Over Tasmania,** Fithian Press), 1997, **Blue Damsels**, (Peter Randall Press), 2005, and **Night Call**, (Plain View Press), 2011. His work has appeared in many magazines. He is an adult and child psychoanalyst and an Associate Clinical Professor of Psychiatry at Harvard University Medical School Massachusetts General Hospital.

Made in the USA
Columbia, SC
16 December 2020